Whose

MW01165252

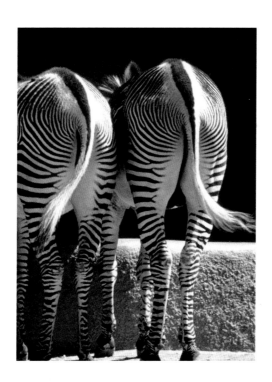

written by Pam Holden

1

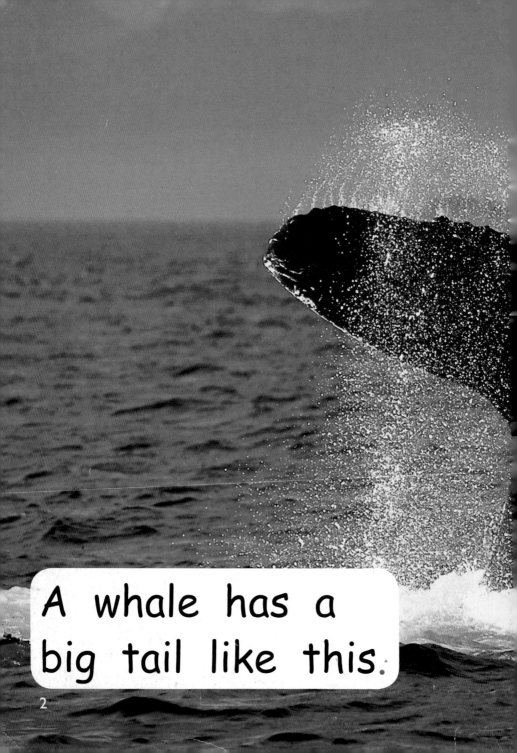

A whale has a
big tail like this.

2

whale

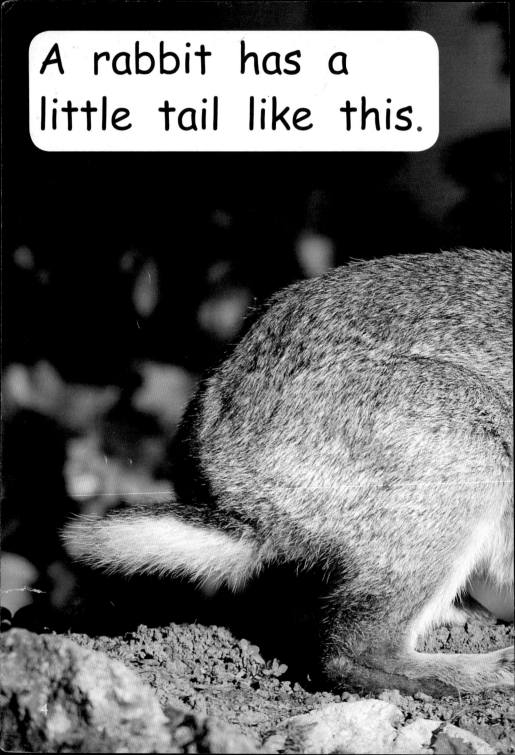

A rabbit has a little tail like this.

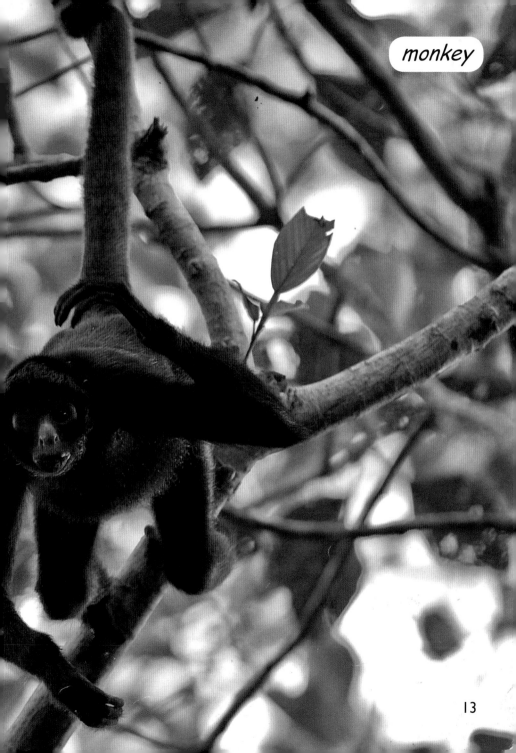

monkey

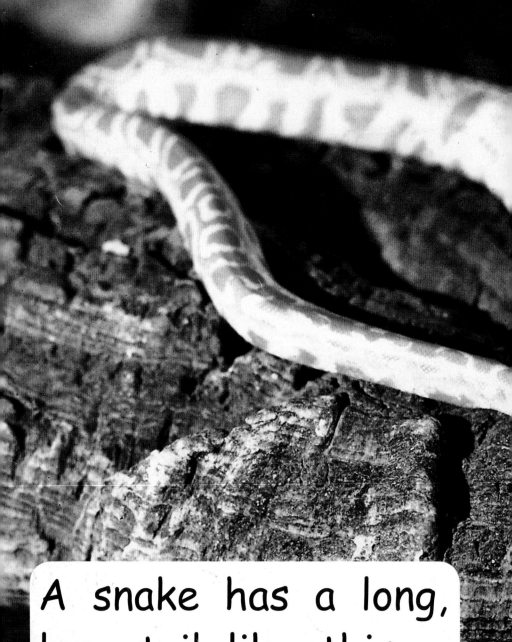

A snake has a long, long tail like this.

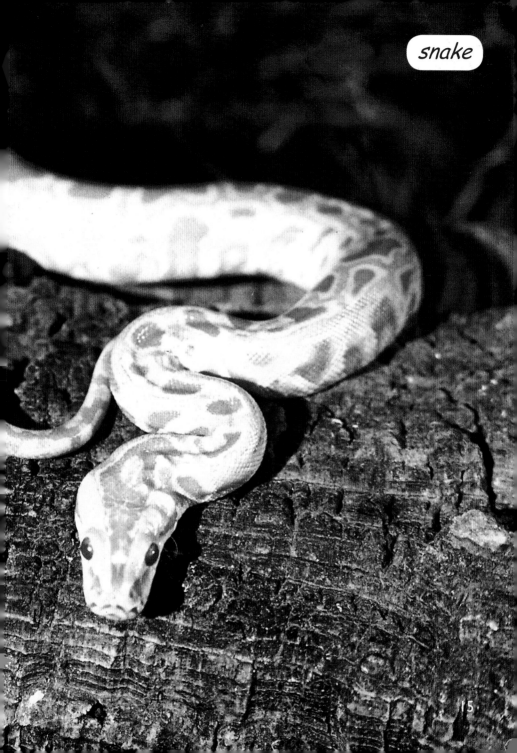

snake

A tiger has a long tail, too. Grrr!

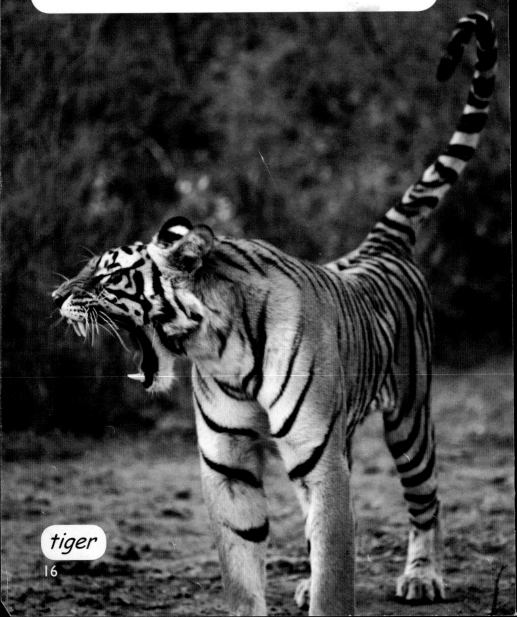

tiger

16